Rooted Together

A FAMILY DEVOTIONAL TO HELP
BUILD A LONG-LASTING RELATIONSHIP
WITH GOD AND EACH OTHER

Kailey Lentsch
Triune Publications

This Devotional Belongs To:

_____

_____

_____

_____

_____

As a special thank you, we would love to offer you this free gift. And hope that it will be a blessing to you.

Scan me

Contents

INTRODUCTION AND HOW TO USE THIS BOOK

Welcome! I am so glad you have found this family devotional. Over the next year, you and your family will study the Bible in a way that lays the foundation for spiritual and relational growth. Each week you will explore and apply Scripture to cultivate loving and long-lasting relationships with one another and with God.

Family is important to God. In the very beginning of the Bible, in the Book of Genesis, we learn that God created the first family. He created both man and woman in His image, yet distinct from one another, and appointed specific roles to each family member. Children were a part of God's plan for the family – in Genesis 1:28 God said, "Be fruitful, multiply, fill the earth…" When we consider the first family, we see that God defines a family as one man and one woman, united in marriage, and their children.

However, sin and brokenness entered the world, and this isn't what all families look like. Relationships are broken, family members are hurtful to one another, and family can be plain messy. The purpose of this book is not to condemn or judge families that look different from the way God intended families to look, rather to help families grow in their love for one another, and for God, by using Scripture as a guide.

"Love is patient, love is kind. Love does not envy, is not boastful, is not arrogant, is not rude, is not self-seeking, is not irritable, and does not keep a record of wrongs. Love finds no joy in unrighteousness but rejoices in the truth. It bears all things, believes all things, hopes all things, endures all things. Love never ends."
1 Corinthians 13:4-8

Isn't this what we want for our families? A kind of love that never ends. Love that is kind, selfless, forgiving, joyful, and enduring. Love that produces faith and hope. These are the core values essential to Christian families who want to grow in their relationships with one another and with God. In His wisdom and grace, God has put these values on display throughout His Story so that we can learn from them.

The devotionals in this book have been categorized into six themes based on the characteristics of love found in 1 Corinthians 13:4-8. At the beginning of each week, you will notice a color and symbol that indicate which theme you will be studying.

The devotionals in this category will focus on love for God and love for your family, and will include scripture on concepts such as compassion, empathy, and forgiveness.

This category highlights scripture to help your family cultivate joy. You will consider how you enjoy one another, God, and creation, as well as how gratitude and praise impact joy.

The respect category will look at how your family can show respect to one another by listening and being honest, patient, loyal, and humble.

The devotionals in this category focus on your relationship with God and will consider Christian practices like prayer, bible study, stewardship, obedience, and steadfastness.

This category highlights scripture to help you get through the trials of life. You will contemplate perseverance, hope, courage, strength, and encouragement.

Evangelism

The evangelism category will explore how your family can be a light to those around you and considers serving, hospitality, generosity, and justice.

Each weekly devotional will consist of five parts:

1. **Read It** – one or two verses from God's Word to be read together as a family.

2. **Think About It** – a brief explanation of the assigned scripture reading and how it applies to your family.

3. **Talk About It** – questions or prompts to help engage you and your family in meaningful conversations about God's Word.

4. **Apply It** – practical, fun ideas to help you and your family live out what you have learned each week or deepen your conversation.

5. **Rank It** – At the end of each devotional, you will see five stars where you and your family can rank how you did on the application.

Before you begin the devotional each week, I encourage you to take time to pray together as a family. This is my prayer for each family reading this devotional:

Father, I pray that you would open the hearts and minds of each member of the family that is reading this devotional. Help them understand your Word and remain engaged throughout this study. I ask that you bless their conversations so that they would be fruitful and bring glory to your name. I pray that you would break down any barriers in this family so that their time together would be productive and so each person feels safe to be open and real. Lord, most of all, I pray that this family would experience joy in being in your Word together and would grow in their love and affection for one another and for you. In Jesus' name, amen.

In the beginning God created the heavens and the earth.

Genesis 1:1

Week 1:

Creativity

Read It

> *In the beginning God created the heavens and the earth.*
> *Genesis 1:1*

Think About It

The Bible begins with the story of creation. Have you ever been given a blank piece of paper and told to make something out of it or to draw a picture on it? Sometimes it can be hard to get our imaginations working and come up with an idea. But God's imagination and power are unlimited – He started with nothing, and from nothing He created everything! God imagined the twinkling stars and spinning planets, the zebra's stripes and the giraffe's long neck, the pattern of honeycomb and your unique thumbprint. When God created humans, He created them in His image (Genesis 1:26). That means we were designed to reflect God – His goodness, kindness, love, grace, and His creativity. God wants us to enjoy His creation and find joy in being creative!

Talk About It

What do you enjoy most about God's creation? How do you like to be creative?

Apply It

Take time as a family to enjoy being in and inspired by God's creation then be creative together. Below are some ideas.

- Go for a walk/hike then make a collage of the nature items you collected
- Paint rocks and hide them around a local park
- Go to the beach and paint seashells or build a sandcastle
- Go stargazing or cloud watching and try to make images or shapes out of the stars or clouds
- Go to a zoo or aquarium then paint or draw pictures of your favorite animals

How did you do with the Apply It for Week 1?

NOTES

So God created man in his own image; he created him in the image of God; he created them male and female.

Genesis 1:27

Week 2:
Everyone is Special to God

Read It

> So God created man in his own image; he created
> him in the image of God;
> he created them male and female.
> *Genesis 1:27*

Think About It

God purposely made humans to resemble His character. This means it doesn't matter what someone looks like, how old they are, if they are a boy or girl, if they are able-bodied or not, or what kind of family they come from, every person was made in God's image. God cares deeply about *all* of His creation, and we should too!

Part of being made in God's image means that we have the ability to act the way God would act. His goodness, kindness, mercy, and love exist in all of us, so we have the power to choose kindness and treat people with compassion. Sometimes this is hard to do, especially with the people closest to us. When we are around someone all the time, it becomes easier to see their mistakes or all the little habits they have that annoy us. But Jesus perfectly modeled how we should treat others. He didn't look at what people looked like on the outside, He looked at their hearts. He didn't focus on the mistakes people made, instead He looked for the good in people. When we choose to look for the good in others instead of focusing on their mistakes or annoying habits, we are able to see them the way God sees them – a valued part of God's creation, made specially in His image.

Talk About It

How do you think your attitude towards others would change if you focused on how they resemble God's character rather than focusing on their flaws?

Apply It

Practice viewing each member of your family as an image-bearer by recognizing godly character traits. For example, "when you helped your sister with her homework you showed kindness like Jesus" or "when you forgave mom for yelling at you, you showed grace like Jesus."

How did you do with the Apply It for Week 2?

NOTES

Two are better than one because they have a good reward for their efforts. For if either falls, his companion can lift him up; but pity the one who falls without another to lift him up.

Ecclesiastes 4:9-10

Week 3:
Created for Relationships

Read It

> *Two are better than one because they have a good reward for their efforts. For if either falls, his companion can lift him up; but pity the one who falls without another to lift him up.*
> *Ecclesiastes 4:9-10*

Think About It

We were created to be in community with God and with each other. God wants us to enjoy and delight in Him just as He enjoys and delights in us as His children. He also wants us to enjoy our earthly relationships between our family members, friends, coworkers, classmates, neighbors, church family, and more! Because there is sin in the world, sometimes relationships are hard. We've all felt the sting of a harsh word or the sadness of feeling lonely. But it was never a part of God's plan for us to be alone. We were made to be helpers – to pick each other up when we fall, to show grace and love to one another, to welcome others into our homes, and to serve one another. When we do this, we glorify God by living out His good purpose for our lives.

Talk About It

What do you enjoy most about your relationship with your family? What is hard for you in your relationships?

Apply It

Plan a night this week to do something enjoyable as a family.

Ideas:

- Plan a family game or movie night

- Go on a picnic

- Play a sport together

- Plan a "mismatched dinner" where each family members gets to pick out one item for dinner (This is one of my family's favorite things to do! We always have so much fun and a lot of laughs when we see what everyone picked out.)

How did you do with the Apply It for Week 3?

NOTES

Wives, submit to your husbands as to the Lord....Husbands, love your wives, just as Christ loved the church and gave himself for her.

Ephesians 5:22, 25

Week 4:

Marriage is an Example

Read It

> *Wives, submit to your husbands as to the Lord...Husbands, love your wives, just as Christ loved the church and gave himself for her.*
> *Ephesians 5:22, 25*

Think About It

God created marriage as a special kind of relationship between a man and a woman. It is an intimate form of companionship, but it is also a reflection of Christ and the church. A man is supposed to love his wife like Jesus loved His church. Jesus sacrificed His life so that the church would be made holy and blameless before God. A husband should help his wife grow closer to Jesus. A woman should love her husband the way the church loves Jesus. As Christians, we should obey God in response to His love for us. Similarly, a wife should submit to her husband, not because she *has* to, but because she trusts that her husband wants what is best for her. For marriage to be an example of Jesus and the church, a husband and a wife both must put each other's needs first. They are willing to give up what they want in order to do what is best for their family.

Talk About It

How is your marriage like Jesus and the church? Ask the kids to give examples too.

Apply It

Reminisce on your wedding day. Watch a wedding video, look through a wedding album, or read your vows with your children.

How did you do with the Apply It for Week 4?

☆ ☆ ☆ ☆ ☆

NOTES

I will put hostility between you and the woman, and between your offspring and her offspring. He will strike your head, and you will strike his heel.

Genesis 3:15

Week 5:

Jesus Already Won

Read It

> *I will put hostility between you and the woman, and between your offspring and her offspring. He will strike your head, and you will strike his heel.*
> *Genesis 3:15*

Think About It

Genesis 3:15 isn't about a fear of snakes or just about the struggle between humans and Satan. It is the first hint of the good work of Christ. Genesis 1-2 (two pages in most Bibles!) describe God's perfect creation. Then, in Genesis 3, sin and brokenness enter the world. In verses 14-19, God lists the curses that will plague all of humanity – pain, broken relationships, difficult work, and separation from God. The rest of the story of the Bible is about restoration – God's perfect plan to fix the problem of sin and make a way to be with

His people again. Even in the garden, God had a plan to rescue His wonderful creation.

We can see now that Jesus was the plan. Satan struck the heel of Jesus when He died on the cross, but Jesus struck the head of Satan three days later when He rose from the grave, conquering all sin and death! However, we are living in an odd period of "already but not yet." Jesus has already struck the serpent's head, yet we still live in a fallen and broken world. Jesus promises to prepare a place for us and to come back one day to take us there with Him. This is the hope we hold on to as we live in the "already but not yet."

Talk About It

How has sin and brokenness impacted your family – what are you most looking forward to seeing made new? For example, there won't be any cancer or bullies in Heaven.

Apply It

Drawing Contest: Use Genesis 3:15 as inspiration and draw a picture to represent this verse. Vote on the best picture and talk about why you liked it.

How did you do with the Apply It for Week 5?

☆ ☆ ☆ ☆ ☆

NOTES

And Noah did this. He did everything that God had commanded him.

Genesis 6:22

Week 6:

Obey Like Noah

Read It

> *And Noah did this. He did everything that*
> *God had commanded him.*
> *Genesis 6:22*

Think About It

After the fall, wickedness and evil overtook the world. God was greatly saddened that His most precious creation had turned against Him. He wanted to give the world a fresh beginning by cleansing the earth with water. He caused a great flood to cover the whole earth, wiping out everything! God chose one man, Noah, to build a giant boat so he and his family, and two of every animal could make it through the flood safely. Can you imagine God telling you there was going to be a flood and you needed to build an ark? How would you have felt if you started to build the ark, but people made fun of you like they did to Noah? And on top of that, how crazy would it seem if God told you to bring two of every animal on this boat with you? Even though it didn't seem to make sense, Noah obeyed God and did all that all that God asked him to do.

God is a good Father, and like a good father does, He gives us instructions to help us make good choices. Sometimes His instructions don't seem to make sense to us in the moment; like when God tells us to move or go to a new school, to change the friends we hang around with, or behave differently from the people around us. We have the example of Noah's faith and how his obedience to God kept him safe and allowed him to make choices that pleased God. The same is true for us, even when it seems like God is telling us something crazy or impossible, we can trust that He knows what is best for us and follow Him faithfully and obediently.

Talk About It

Has God ever told your family to do something that didn't seem to make sense? How did you handle it?

Apply It

Practice obedience by playing a game of Simon Says. Get creative and have tasks that don't make sense like do a handstand, eat dessert before dinner, read a book upside down. Have a little reward for the winner and remind your family that just like Noah, even when things don't make sense, we are blessed for our obedience.

How did you do with the Apply It for Week 6?

NOTES

I am the door. If anyone enters by me, he will be saved and will go in and out and find pasture.

John 10:9

Week 7:

God's Way

Read It

> *I am the door. If anyone enters by me, he will be saved and will go in and out and find pasture.*
> *John 10:9*

Think About It

Have you ever gone to an escape room? In order to "escape" the room, you must solve riddles or find clues that lead you to the exit. Each riddle has only one correct answer and if you don't find it, you lose the game. Once Noah built the ark, there was only one way in, and God Himself shut the door behind him. God gave Noah specific instructions and because Noah obeyed God, he was saved from the flood.

Jesus says He is the door, the only way we can be saved from sin. The world will tell us that happiness or money or popularity are all we need, but if we want to go to Heaven, we can only get there through Jesus. Even our own good works aren't enough! We must have faith and trust that Jesus will do what He has promised to do. In response to His love and grace, we should obey Him.

Talk About It

Have you ever felt like you needed more 'stuff' or needed to 'do more' or 'be better' to earn your way to Heaven? What does it mean that Jesus is 'the door'?

Apply It

Go to an escape room or make your own at home!

How did you do with the Apply It for Week 7?

NOTES

...and there was a vast multitude from every nation, tribe, people and language, which no one could number, standing before the throne and before the Lamb.

Revelation 7:9

Evangelism

Week 8:

Sin Divides,
Jesus Unites

Read It

> *…and there was a vast multitude from every nation, tribe, people, and language, which no one could number, standing before the throne and before the Lamb.*
> Revelation 7:9

Think About It

In the story of the Tower of Babel, the people thought they were important and could be like God so they set out to build a tower to the heavens to make a name for themselves. However, because of their pride, God scattered the people and confused their languages. Sin always has consequences and often it causes divisions among people. In Acts 2, God does the complete opposite of what He did at Babel – God sent the Holy Spirit to allow the apostles to speak in tongues and proclaim the gospel in other languages. People from all over the known world learned about Jesus and were united on this amazing day!

Sin divides but Jesus unites. Heaven will be full of different kinds of people and God gives us unique gifts and talents so that we can share the gospel with people we might not normally talk to. Maybe you're really good at a sport and meet new friends on your team. Perhaps you're a people person and can strike up a conversation with your server or cashier. No matter how significant or insignificant a talent or gift may seem, God can use it to help others come to know Jesus.

Talk About It

Who are the people you've met through random circumstances that you wouldn't normally interact with or know otherwise? Do you think God brought those people in your life so you could share the Good News of Jesus Christ with them?

Apply It

Serve a group of people you don't normally interact with.

Ideas: volunteer at a local soup kitchen or food pantry, become pen pals with a family from another country/culture or someone who is incarcerated, shop at a store in an area of town you don't usually go.

How did you do with the Apply It for Week 8?

NOTES

He will reign over the house of Jacob forever, and his kingdom will have no end.

Luke 1:33

ENDURANCE

Waiting

Read It

> *He will reign over the house of Jacob forever, and his kingdom will have no end.*
> *Luke 1:33*

Think About It

God promised Abraham that he would not only have a son, but that he would be made into a great nation, with as many descendants as stars in the sky. This promise seemed ridiculous because Abraham was very old, but he believed God and had faith that God would keep His promise. Abraham waited 25 years for God to fulfill this promise! In those 25 years he made mistakes and tried to do things his way instead of waiting on God. Even still, God was faithful to keep His promise.

The prophets spoke of a coming Messiah, the One who would rule forever. There was great hope in their message and the people longed for the Messiah to come. But like Abraham, they had to wait for God to fulfill His promise to send a Savior. It was over 400 years from the time the last prophet spoke to when the angel announced the coming Messiah!

Sometimes we have to wait for God, but we can trust that God always keeps His promises. Luke 1:33 tells us that Jesus will rule forever, and His kingdom will never end. We can persevere through the seasons of waiting because we have the hope of eternity with Jesus. When we focus on eternity, waiting for a day, a week, a year, or even 25 years seems short in comparison.

Talk About It

Have you ever had to wait for something you really wanted? How did you feel?

Apply It

Make bread together. Mix up two batches of dough. Cook one immediately but let the other batch sit and rise according to the directions. Once the two loafs are baked, compare how they look, how they taste, and their texture. Remind you family that when we are impatient and don't do things God's way things can get messy or ugly like the dough that didn't rise. When we wait for God and trust in Him, things are more beautiful than we could ever imagine!

How did you do with the Apply It for Week 9?

NOTES

For we do not have a high priest who is unable to sympathize with our weaknesses, but one who has been tempted in every way as we are, yet without sin. Therefore, let us approach the throne of grace with boldness, so that we may receive mercy and find grace to help us in time of need.

Hebrews 4:15-16

Week 10:
God Wants Us to Come to Him

Read It

> *For we do not have a high priest who is unable to sympathize with our weaknesses, but one who has been tempted in every way as we are, yet without sin. Therefore, let us approach the throne of grace with boldness, so that we may receive mercy and find grace to help us in time of need.*
> *Hebrews 4:15-16*

Think About It

God wants to be with His people! Before Jesus came, only the priests were allowed to enter the holy part of the temple and God only spoke through prophets, visions, or angels. God wants us to be able to come to Him but because of sin, we are separated from God. Jesus is the solution to our separation from God — He loves us so much that He made a way for us to be with our Father again.

We never have to be afraid or embarrassed to go to God because Jesus experienced the same struggles and temptations that we face. We can go to God confidently with our struggles and know that He will help us. We can even go to Him with our sin and know that He will never stop loving us or pouring out His grace on us.

Talk About It

How can we be with God now, on this side of Heaven?

Apply It

Create a prayer jar. Jesus made a way for us to talk to God and be near Him right now and that is through prayer. As a family, brainstorm things that you can pray to God about – it could be things to thank God for, praises, requests, etc. Write down some of these things on craft sticks and put them in a jar or vase. Throughout the week take turns pulling out a stick and praying for whatever is written on it.

How did you do with the Apply It for Week 10?

NOTES

Then Peter approached him and asked, "Lord, how many times must I forgive my brother or sister who sins against me? As many as seven times?"

"I tell you, not as many as seven," Jesus replied,

"but seventy times seven."

Matthew 18:21-22

Week 11:
Forgive Like Jesus Forgave You

Read It

> *Then Peter approached him and asked, "Lord, how many times must I forgive my brother or sister who sins against me? As many as seven times?" "I tell you, not as many as seven," Jesus replied, "but seventy times seven."*
> *Matthew 18:21-22*

Think About It

Joseph's brothers plotted to kill him, but he was sold into slavery and taken to Egypt instead. There, he was falsely accused and put in jail. While he was in jail, he earned trust and respect and rose as a leader in Egypt. He eventually used his role to save his family from a famine. Joseph's brothers were afraid that Joseph would hold a grudge and want to punish them. Instead, Joseph offered them forgiveness and comforted them. In Genesis 50:20, Joseph says, "You planned evil against me; God planned it for good to bring about the present result – the survival of many people."

Similarly, Jesus was plotted against. Many people hated Jesus and wanted Him dead. They falsely accused Him and gave Him a rigged trial to find Him guilty. Although they killed Jesus, He rose as the ruler of the world and conqueror over all sin and death. Jesus used his role to save the entire world from sin. He offers us grace and forgiveness that we could never deserve and asks His Father to forgive us.

Just like Joseph and Jesus gave others forgiveness, we should be willing to forgive those who hurt us. This can be a hard thing to do! But many times, when we are unwilling to forgive someone, it upsets us more than the person who hurt us. When we forgive others, we let go of the negative feelings we have towards someone and instead focus on the love and grace Christ has for us. This turns our hearts from bitterness to thankfulness.

Talk About It

Do you think you would have been able to forgive your brothers if you were Joseph? Why is it hard to forgive others sometimes?

Apply It

Act it out. Think about some recent scenarios where each person in your family was slow to forgive or hasn't yet extended forgiveness. Take turns acting out the situations and what you could have done differently to show forgiveness.

How did you do with the Apply It for Week 11?

NOTES

God replied to Moses, "I AM WHO I AM. This is what you are to say to the Israelites: I AM has sent me to you."

Exodus 3:14

Week 12:

I AM

Read It

> *God replied to Moses, "I AM WHO I AM. This is what you are to say to the Israelites: I AM has sent me to you."*
> *Exodus 3:14*

Think About It

God told Moses His name was "I AM". This may seem strange, but by saying, "I am who I am", God is telling Moses, *there aren't enough words or a name encompassing enough to describe who I am.* We truly cannot fathom all that God is and that should cause us to pause and marvel at His majesty.

In John 8:58, Jesus says, "before Abraham was, I AM." The Jews are so offended by this, they want to stone Him. They understood that Jesus was saying He was God. They were too blinded by their pride to see who Jesus really was. Sometimes we can be blinded by the things of this world and take for granted or miss who Jesus is. He is the great I AM. He is the Savior of the World, Wonderful Counselor, Mighty God, Eternal Father, and Prince of Peace (Isaiah 9:6).

Talk About It

Sometimes we think of Jesus as our Savior and forget to think of Him as our friend, or we know Him as Lord but not as Redeemer. Are there any characteristics you tend to forget, ignore, or miss when it comes to Jesus? How can you try to remember all that Jesus is?

Apply It

Make a list of the characteristics of God. Try to find one word that represents all of the characteristics you wrote down. Do you think "I AM" is an accurate name? Spend time praising God for being all these things!

How did you do with the Apply It for Week 12?

NOTES

Don't worry about anything, but in everything, through prayer and petition with thanksgiving, present your requests to God. And the peace of God, which surpasses all understanding, will guard your hearts and minds in Christ Jesus.

Philippians 4:6-7

Week 13:

We Can Be Happy with What We Have

Read It

> *Don't worry about anything, but in everything, through prayer and petition with thanksgiving, present your requests to God. And the peace of God, which surpasses all understanding, will guard your hearts and minds in Christ Jesus.*
> *Philippians 4:6-7*

Think About It

God had delivered the entire Israelite nation out of slavery. He had performed many signs and wonders and even after all that, the Israelites complained. God, in His kindness and grace, provided them with manna, bread that rained down from Heaven. Each person was able to gather what they could eat. Yet, even after this provision, the Israelites began to complain about the manna and wanted other food to eat. Instead of being grateful for God's provision, they were discontent.

Discontentment steals our joy and leaves us feeling empty, always longing for more. The truth is, Jesus is the only one who can truly satisfy us. One of the lines in the Lord's Prayer is "give us this day our daily bread." We learn from this line that it is appropriate to go to our Father with our needs and requests, but we should do so with humility and gratitude for His provision. God will give us what we need and what we need the most is Jesus!

Talk About It

What areas of your life do you struggle with discontentment? Examples: money, clothes, games/toys, house, type of car, physical appearance, athletic ability, school performance, etc.

Apply It

Fast together. A fast is a temporary break from something in order to focus your attention on God. We see fasting a lot in the Old Testament. People would not eat for a period of time so their physical bodies would be as uncomfortable as they felt spiritually and emotionally. When they felt hunger pangs, it was a reminder to go to God in prayer. Today, people fast in different ways. They may take a break from social media, eating out, spending, sweets, caffeine, etc. Make a commitment to fast together this week. You can all pick the same thing or something different but encourage and check in with one another throughout the week.

How did you do with the Apply It for Week 13?

NOTES

For the whole law is fulfilled in one statement: Love your neighbor as yourself.

Galatians 5:14

Week 14:
Love Your Neighbor as Yourself

Read It

> *For the whole law is fulfilled in one statement: Love your neighbor as yourself.*
> *Galatians 5:14*

Think About It

We often think of the "Law" as the Ten Commandments, but there were 613 laws given to the Israelites! Laws about sacrifices and festivals, how to treat other Israelites, and how to treat foreigners. It was impossible to keep all of these laws, and the sacrificial system was put in place as a way for the Israelites to atone for their sins. As if 613 laws weren't hard enough to try to keep, the Pharisees added extra rules for the Jewish people to follow. These extra rules were supposed to help them keep the 613 laws, but it became a burden that no human could bear.

In Matthew 5, Jesus gives a "new commandment" which seems to make the Law even more difficult to keep! Now, "do not murder" becomes "don't hate someone or you have murdered them in your heart" and "do not commit adultery" becomes "do not even look at someone lustfully." Galatians 5:14 says, "For the whole law is fulfilled in one statement: Love your neighbor as yourself." All 613 laws can be summed up and fulfilled by loving others. When your family loves others together, it not only helps someone else, but it strengthens your love with one another too.

Talk About It

Who is your 'neighbor' and what are some ways you can love your neighbor?

Apply It

Obey God's command to love your neighbors this week.

Ideas: help a neighbor with yard work, pick up trash at your local park, send a care package to someone, mail a card or send an encouraging text to someone who is going through a hard time, take cookies to a nursing home.

How did you do with the Apply It for Week 14?

NOTES

But in every nation the person who fears him and does what is right is acceptable to him.

Acts 10:35

Evangelism

Read It

> *But in every nation the person who fears him and does what is right is acceptable to him.*
> *Acts 10:35*

Think About It

There were a lot of rules about what the Israelites could or could not eat. God's people were supposed to be pure and holy like God was pure and holy, so they could not put anything that God deemed as unclean into their bodies. They couldn't even be around people who ate something unclean! In Acts 10, Peter has a vision in which the Lord tells him to hunt and eat unclean animals. Peter is shocked and says he would never do such a thing! But God rebukes Peter and tells him not to call anything unclean that He has made clean. Peter later realizes that this vision was to show him that the gospel was not just for Jews, but for Gentiles as well.

71

Sometimes we may look at someone and think they are too mean, have made too many mistakes, or are too lost for God to save them. But God is powerful enough to change even the hardest of hearts. Jesus is for everyone.

Talk About It

Have you ever thought someone was too "unclean" or too sinful to be saved? What made you think that?

Apply It

God is mighty enough to save *anyone*. Commit to praying for God to work in the hearts of the following people this week.

Monday: The incarcerated

Tuesday: Those struggling with addiction

Wednesday: Atheist

Thursday: Those who are devoted to another religion

Friday: People who abuse and mistreat others

How did you do with the Apply It for Week 15?

NOTES

The Word became flesh and dwelt among us. We observed his glory, the glory of the one and only Son from the Father, full of grace and truth.

John 1:14

Week 16:

Enjoy Being with God

Read It

> *The Word became flesh and dwelt among us. We observed his glory, the glory of the one and only Son from the Father, full of grace and truth.*
> *John 1:14*

Think About It

In the Old Testament, the tabernacle was the dwelling place of God. It created a way for the Lord to be with His people. However, it had major limitations – sacrifices were required and only the priests were allowed in on the people's behalf. When Jesus came to earth, He took away all those limitations. He was God in the flesh, dwelling (or tabernacling) with His creation.

Today we have access to God through the Holy Spirit. God wants to be with His people! God wants to be with *you*! You don't have to rely on a priest or a sacrifice, you have full access to God, and He wants you to enjoy being in His presence. He wants you to feel His peace, comfort, love, and joy and know that you are never alone. Sometimes we feel God's presence when we read His Word or when we pray. Other times we feel God's nearness when we are with other people who love Him or when we spend time in His creation. God has given us many ways to enjoy His presence.

Talk About It

What are some ways you can enjoy being with God?

Apply It

Build a "tabernacle" fort. Gather blankets, pillows, furniture, and whatever else you need and work together to build an epic fort. Enjoy being together in your fort and enjoy being with God.

How did you do with the Apply It for Week 16?

NOTES

Children, obey your parents in the Lord, because this is right. Honor your father and mother, which is the first commandment with a promise, so that it may go well with you and that you may have long life in the land.

Ephesians 6:1-3

Week 17:
Honor Your Father and Mother

Read It

> *Children, obey your parents in the Lord, because this is right. Honor your father and mother, which is the first commandment with a promise, so that it may go well with you and that you may have long life in the land.*
> *Ephesians 6:1-3*

Think About It

One of the Ten Commandments is honor your father and mother. The way we treat our parents is important to God, so important that He commands us to treat them with respect. This command comes with a promise: honor your parents *so that it may go well with you.* A parent's job is to help their children grow and learn in a way that is healthy and safe. To do that, parents must give their children rules. Sometimes you may see how a rule is for your safety, like look both ways before you cross the street. Other times, you may not understand why your parents have a certain rule. Even if you don't understand or agree with the rule, God says we should obey our parents. God has specifically chosen your parents for you, and you for your parents. You can respect His plan by obeying your parents. This pleases your parents, but more importantly, it pleases God.

Talk About It

Are there any rules in your family you don't understand or disagree with? Parents, help your children understand why these rules are important. Is there any room for compromise?

Apply It

Play a game of What If? Take turns giving a scenario, "What if we broke _____ rule?" then the other family members build on the scenario to create a fun story of what could happen. It's OK to be silly, but the point is to see how rules keep us safe, physically and spiritually.

How did you do with the Apply It for Week 17?

NOTES

Haven't I commanded you:
be strong and
courageous? Do not
be afraid or
discouraged, for
the Lord your God
is with you
wherever you go."
Joshua 1:9

Week 18:

Brave Like Joshua

Read It

> *Haven't I commanded you: be strong and courageous?*
> *Do not be afraid or discouraged, for the Lord your*
> *God is with you wherever you go."*
> *Joshua 1:9*

Think About It

Joshua was the man God chose to replace Moses when Moses died. He would be tasked with leading the Israelites in many battles and into the Promised Land. Although this wasn't an easy job, Joshua had courage and was confident in how he led the people because God promised to always be with him. Joshua was able to encourage the Israelites to be brave and courageous too by reminding them that God was on their side.

Parents are given a job like Joshua, to look after, lead, and encourage their children. Sometimes your family will face scary or hard things, but God's promise to Joshua and the Israelites is true for your family too – God is always with you. As parents rely on God to strengthen and encourage them, they are able to strengthen and encourage their children to face the battles of life.

Talk About It

What are some ways parents can help their children feel brave when they face scary or difficult situations?

Apply It

Face a fear together! Ideas: practice swimming, pet a snake, read out loud in Bible class, lead a prayer at church.

How did you do with the Apply It for Week 18?

NOTES

But if it doesn't please you to worship the Lord, choose for yourselves today: Which will you worship — the gods your ancestors worshiped beyond the Euphrates River or the gods of the Amorites in whose land you are living? As for me and my family, we will worship the Lord."

Joshua 24:15

Week 19:

Commit to the Lord

Read It

> But if it doesn't please you to worship the Lord, choose for yourselves today: Which will you worship – the gods your ancestors worshiped beyond the Euphrates River or the gods of the Amorites in whose land you are living? As for me and my family, we will worship the Lord."
>
> Joshua 24:15

Think About It

Even after the Israelites made it into the Promised Land, Joshua understood that their obedience and commitment to God would be necessary for them to be successful. It would have been easier for the people to go back to worshipping idols who didn't give them so many rules or require so many sacrifices, but that's not what would have been best for them.

Sometimes being a Christian can be hard, but we must choose – either we serve God, or we don't. There is no in-between or room to be wishy-washy. We must love the Lord with all our heart, all our soul and all our mind (Matthew 22:37). Joshua's commitment to the Lord wasn't just about himself, his whole family was committed to putting God first. When we commit our lives to God as a family, it is easier to make Him the priority because our decisions are based on what God wants for us, not what we want.

Talk About It

Are there any ways that your family is not committed to worshipping God? For example, is there anything you view more important to do on Sundays instead of going to church? When at church are you focused on the lesson? Do you make decisions based on God's Word or based on what you want?

Apply It

Commit to serving the Lord in one way this week. Has it been a while since you've gone to church? Make it a priority to go this Sunday. Do you put off reading your Bible? Set aside time each day this week to read a couple verses as a family.

How did you do with the Apply It for Week 19?

NOTES

Don't plead with me to abandon you or to return and not follow you. For wherever you go, I will go, and wherever you live, I will live; your people will be my people, and your God will be my God.

Ruth 1:16

Week 20:
Commit to Your Family

Read It

> *Don't plead with me to abandon you or to return and not follow you. For wherever you go, I will go, and wherever you live, I will live; your people will be my people, and your God will be my God.*
> *Ruth 1:16*

Think About It

The Bible tells a story about a woman named Naomi whose husband and two sons died. Her sons had married but never had children. Naomi thought it was best for her two daughters-in-law to return to their families and remarry. One of them did, but the other daughter-in-law, Ruth, refused to leave Naomi. Ruth showed great love, concern, and respect to Naomi by choosing to remain with her. Ruth goes on to work in the fields to provide for Naomi and herself and she obeys Naomi's requests. Even though Ruth no longer had any obligation to Naomi, she remained loyally by her side and never stopped helping or loving her.

91

This is the kind of loyalty and commitment God wants us to have towards the family He has given us. Sometimes it may seem easier to avoid or ignore each other when conflict or difficult circumstances arise but in the long run it's always better to face those things together. We should always be looking for ways to help and love our family so that we grow closer together and strengthen our relationships with one another.

Talk About It

How does your family handle conflict or difficult circumstances? Are any changes needed?

Apply It

Is there a conflict or issue you've been avoiding with your family, extended family, or church family? Don't run away from it, commit to working together to find a resolution.

How did you do with the Apply It for Week 20?

NOTES

But encourage each other daily, while it is still called today, so none of you is hardened by sin's deception. Hebrews 3:13

Week 21:

Encourage One Another

Read It

> But encourage each other daily, while it is still called today, so none of you is hardened by sin's deception.
> *Hebrews 3:13*

Think About It

Naomi was so upset about losing her husband and sons that she changed her name to Mara, which means *bitter*. When life gets hard, Satan has the perfect opportunity to creep in and tempt us. Sometimes this is obvious like when we are sinful in our actions, but other times it is more subtle like when we have negative thoughts and feelings. This is what happened to Naomi. She was bitter towards God for allowing such tragedy in her life. She had all but given up hope until Ruth committed to stay with her. Ruth's faith, obedience, loyalty, and kindness renewed Naomi's hope.

We can be a source of encouragement to our family and to others when they are going through a hard time. Something as simple as a smile or saying, "I'm praying for you" may be all it takes to renew someone's hope and help them withstand temptation.

Talk About It

Take turns talking about what is most encouraging to you when you are going through something hard so your family knows how to best help you. Do you like a handwritten note, face-to-face conversations, or a hug? Do you like to talk about things right away or do you need time to think first?

Apply It

Do you know anyone (in your family or not in your family) who is going through a difficult time right now? Choose one way your family can be an encouragement to that person.

Ideas: send a "thinking of you" note in the mail, invite them over, drop off their favorite treat or drink, pray with and for them.

How did you do with the Apply It for Week 21?

NOTES

If you remain in me and my words remain in you, ask whatever you want and it will be done for you.

John 15:7

Week 22:
Ask and You Shall Receive

Read It

> *If you remain in me and my words remain in you,*
> *ask whatever you want and it will be done for you.*
> *John 15:7*

Think About It

Jesus tells us that we can ask for whatever we want, and it will be done for us. That doesn't mean that prayer is like a magical lamp and God is a genie who must grant our wishes. God is always going to do His will and what brings Him the most glory. The key to receiving the things we ask God for is asking for things that align with His will.

A good example of this is Hannah. Hannah was unable to have children, and this made her very sad. She cried out to God and asked for a son. In her prayer, she promised to dedicate her son to work for the Lord, meaning he would live in the temple and not at home with her.

99

God answered Hannah's prayer and she had a son named Samuel. Just as Hannah promised, once Samuel was old enough, she brought him to the temple where he would live. Although Hannah wanted a son to love and care for, her prayer shows that her priority was in glorifying God and doing what was pleasing to Him.

Sometimes we think we know what is best and we don't take the time to look at God's Word for advice or trust that His will is what is truly best for us. The more we pray and read our Bibles, the more we will understand what God's will is. And when we pray according to God's will, whatever we want will be done for us.

Talk About It

How can you know if something is in line with God's will?

Apply It

Talk about things you've prayed for in the past and how God answered those prayers. Was your prayer in line with God's will? Did He say 'yes'? If He said 'no' or 'not yet', how have you seen God use that in your life?

How did you do with the Apply It for Week 22?

NOTES

Why do you look at the splinter in your brother's eye but don't notice the beam of wood in your own eye? Or how can you say to your brother, 'Let me take the splinter out of your eye, and look, there's a beam of wood in your own eye? Hypocrite! First take the beam of wood out of your eye, and then you will see clearly to take the splinter out of your brother's eye.

Matthew 7:3-5

Week 23:
Check Your Own Eyes First

Read It

Why do you look at the splinter in your brother's eye but don't notice the beam of wood in your own eye? Or how can you say to your brother, 'Let me take the splinter out of your eye,' and look, there's a beam of wood in your own eye? Hypocrite! First take the beam of wood out of your eye, and then you will see clearly to take the splinter out of your brother's eye.
Matthew 7:3-5

Think About It

David was a wonderful king for the nation of Israel, but like all of us, he struggled with sin. David had a relationship with a woman who wasn't his wife and then had her husband killed in battle to try to cover up his sin. The prophet Nathan told David a story about a rich man who had many sheep and cattle but stole a poor man's only lamb to prepare for his guest. David was outraged by the story and said the rich man

103

deserved to die. Imagine David's surprise when Nathan said, "you are that man!" David had been trying to hide his sin so long that he acted like it wasn't even there, yet he was quick to recognize the rich man's sin and pass judgement on him.

My husband is an optometrist. If his eyes aren't healthy and seeing well, he is unable to check other people's eyes to make sure they are healthy and seeing well. Even if he gets the tiniest speck of dust in his eye, he must remove it before he can do his patient's eye exam. As a family, it is necessary and appropriate to point out each other's sins so that you can seek forgiveness and learn from your mistakes. However, this should be done with humility, first recognizing our own flaws before you point out someone else's. When you remove the beam in your own eye first, it helps you go to others with compassion rather than judgement and it helps them be willing to listen to you rather than be defensive.

Talk About It

How can you know if something is in line with God's will?

Apply It

Set up an obstacle course. Have two people wear a blindfold. One person will walk through the obstacle course and the other will try to coach or lead them through it. Time yourself to see how long it takes you to complete the course. Now, have the person coaching take off their blindfold and guide the other person through the course again. How much quicker were you the second time?

How did you do with the Apply It for Week 23?

NOTES

Don't you know that your body is a temple of the Holy Spirit who is in you, whom you have from God? You are not your own, for you were bought at a price. So glorify God with your body.

1 Corinthians 6:19-20

Week 24:

Your Body is a Temple

Read It

> *Don't you know that your body is a temple of the Holy*
> *Spirit who is in you, whom you have from God?*
> *You are not your own, for you were bought at a price.*
> *So glorify God with your body.*
> *1 Corinthians 6:19-20*

Think About It

In the Old Testament, God dwelled with His people by having His spirit come down to the tabernacle, a portable place of worship. Solomon wanted God to have a permanent place with His people, so he built a beautiful temple as a place for the people to worship God and offer sacrifices. The temple was made of gold and fine linens and had many ornate decorations. Unfortunately, this temple proved it wasn't permanent when it was destroyed by the Babylonians.

The good news for us is, the New Testament tells us that our own bodies are temples and the dwelling place of God. The Holy Spirit lives in everyone who puts their trust in Jesus. If Solomon took such care in creating a temple, a mere building, for God, how much more should we care for our bodies that the Spirit lives in? Part of being faithful to God is glorifying Him with how we use and treat our bodies.

Talk About It

How can you glorify God with your body?

Apply It

Do an inventory of what your family has put in their bodies this week. What kinds of foods did you eat and what kinds of drinks did you drink? What did you consume visually and auditorily (movies you watched, music you listened to, apps and games you used, etc.) Do you think these things were glorifying to God? Why or why not?

How did you do with the Apply It for Week 24?

NOTES

All Scripture is
inspired by God and
is profitable for
teaching, for rebuking,
for correcting, for
training in
righteousness, so that
the man of God may
be complete, equipped
for every good work.

2 Timothy 3:16-17

Week 25:
Study God's Word

Read It

> *All Scripture is inspired by God and is profitable for teaching, for rebuking, for correcting, for training in righteousness, so that the man of God may be complete, equipped for every good work.*
> *2 Timothy 3:16-17*

Think About It

Ezra was a scribe who was an expert in the Law. He was committed to not just know God's Law, but to practice it and teach it to others. Ezra is a great example of someone who studied God's Word and then also applied it to his life. Knowing our Bible is the only way we can know how God wants us to live our lives. Scripture teaches us what is right, points out where we've been wrong and corrects and trains us to be more like Jesus.

In Matthew 23, Jesus calls out the scribes and pharisees for not practicing what they preached. They were experts in the Law like Ezra was, but unlike Ezra they didn't obey the Law. God says that we must be doers of His Word, not just hearers (James 1:22). We need to be like Ezra and practice what we learn from Scripture.

Talk About It

How does knowing your Bible "equip you for good works"?

Apply It

Choose a verse that is important to your family and commit to memorizing it this week.

How did you do with the Apply It for Week 25?

NOTES

Do nothing out of selfish ambition or conceit, but in humility consider others as more important than yourselves.

Philippians 2:3

Week 26:
Put Others First

Read It

> *Do nothing out of selfish ambition or conceit, but in humility consider others as more important than yourselves.*
> *Philippians 2:3*

Think About It

Nehemiah was a cupbearer for the king and as such, he lived a comfortable and safe life in the city of Susa. When he heard that the walls of Jerusalem, his hometown, had been destroyed, he wept and prayed for the Israelites. Even though Nehemiah no longer lived in Jerusalem, and he wasn't responsible for the wall being destroyed, he took the initiative to go back and rebuild the wall. This certainly wasn't an easy job, Nehemiah was mocked and faced many attacks and attempts to sabotage his work. He had compassion for Israel and wanted to do what was best for the people even if it meant putting himself in danger. Nehemiah showed great humility and selflessness as he led the people in rebuilding the wall.

Hopefully God never asks you to put yourself in danger to help someone else, but there will likely be times in your life that He asks you to put aside the things you want and do what is best for others instead. He may ask a parent to change jobs so they have more time with their children or maybe He wants a brother to give the last cookie to his sister. Whether its big or small, practicing humility by putting others first shows respect and care for them.

Talk About It

What are some ways you can put your family member's needs and desires before your own?

Apply It

Compete with one another for good deeds this week. Who can open the most doors for others? Who can bring in the most grocery bags? Who can fold the most laundry? Remember, we are supposed to *selflessly* care for others, so no prize for the winner this time!

How did you do with the Apply It for Week 26?

NOTES

If you were of the world, the world would love you as its own. However, because you are not of the world, but I have chosen you out of it, the world hates you.

John 15:19

Week 27:
Not of the World

Read It

> *If you were of the world, the world would love you as its own. However, because you are not of the world, but I have chosen you out of it, the world hates you.*
> *John 15:19*

Think About It

Throughout the Bible there are stories of people who stood up for truth and even risked their lives to do what is right. Shadrach, Meshach, and Abednego refused to bow down to the king's golden statue, Mordecai refused to bow down to Haman, Esther refused to remain silent and watch her people be killed, and Daniel refused to quit praying to God. All of these people remained faithful to God by holding fast to their beliefs and values even when they seemed silly or unwise to the rest of the world.

As Christians, our lives should look different from the rest of the world. Unfortunately, if we live counter-culture lives, there will be times that we are made fun of, harassed, or even persecuted for our beliefs. In John 15, Jesus gives us a heads up and tells us this will be the case but just one chapter over, He reminds us that we don't have to be afraid of how the world will treat us because He has overcome the world (John 16:33).

Talk About It

Have you ever been teased or harassed for your Christian beliefs that don't match up with the rest of the world? How did you handle the situation?

Apply It

Have an honest, respectful conversation with each other about where your lives may look more like the world instead of more like Jesus.

How did you do with the Apply It for Week 27?

NOTES

This is the day the Lord has made; let's rejoice and be glad in it.

Psalm 118:24

Week 28:
Find Joy in Each Day

Read It

> *This is the day the Lord has made;*
> *let's rejoice and be glad in it.*
> *Psalm 118:24*

Think About It

God doesn't expect us to be happy all the time or enjoy every moment of our lives. He understands that we go through really hard seasons and struggle with overwhelming emotions at times. But no matter what is going on in our lives, we can always find something to rejoice in. Psalm 118:24 reminds us that we can rejoice simply because God has given us another day. As we practice rejoicing in the little things that we often take for granted, we learn to be more content with what we have. Think about it – God is sustaining your heartbeat at this very moment; He is causing air to fill your lungs. Rejoice and be glad in the life He has given you and trust that He has given you everything you need.

Talk About It

What do you have to be joyful about today?

Apply It

Choose a time each day this week (my family does dinner time) to talk about the highs and lows of your day. Ask each family member what their favorite part of the day was (their high) and what their least favorite part of the day was (their low). Then ask them what brought them joy or made them glad.

How did you do with the Apply It for Week 28?

NOTES

For God will bring
every act to judgment,
including every
hidden thing, whether
good or evil.

Ecclesiastes 12:14

Week 29:

Confess and Repent

Read It

> *For God will bring every act to judgment, including every hidden thing, whether good or evil.*
> *Ecclesiastes 12:14*

Think About It

Confess and repent. These are two words that most people don't really understand, and if they do, they don't like them. That's because talking about our sins and saying we're sorry is hard. However, learning to develop a regular rhythm of confession and repentance is important for every Christian. There are no secrets from God; He knows all and sees all, even those "tiny" sins you think no one else knows about. God is ready to extend forgiveness and shower you with mercy and grace if you would admit your wrongdoings, sincerely apologize, and make every attempt to turn away from your sin.

Learning to confess to God is hard enough, but what can be even more uncomfortable is confessing to other people. Confessing sins to trusted friends or family is so important though because it helps others know how to pray for you, encourage you, and keep you accountable.

Talk About It

Do you all have at least one person you feel like you can confess your sins to who will love and support you?

Apply It

Practice confessing your sins to one another this week. Start with the obvious ones, even if you both know what happened, say it out loud. As you push through the awkwardness of this, you will begin to feel more comfortable confessing sin and asking for help when you are feeling tempted.

How did you do with the Apply It for Week 29?

NOTES

Go, therefore, and make disciples of all nations, baptizing them in the name of the Father and of the Son and of the Holy Spirit, teaching them to observe everything I have commanded you. And remember, I am with you always, to the end of the age.

Matthew 28:19-20

Evangelism

Go and Tell

Read It

> Go, therefore, and make disciples of all nations, baptizing
> them in the name of the Father and of the Son and of the
> Holy Spirit, teaching them to observe everything I have
> commanded you. And remember, I am with you always,
> to the end of the age.
> Matthew 28:19-20

Think About It

If you read through the stories of the prophets in the Bible, you will see how God called and equipped each of them to share His message with other people. As Christians, we are called to share the message of the Gospel. This can seem like a huge, intimidating, and even impossible task and we often feel underqualified to do the job. In Matthew 28, Jesus gave His disciples a command to tell others about Him and His last words before He ascended to Heaven were, "And remember, I am with you always." We can have confidence in sharing Jesus with others because He

131

is with us. He calls us and equips us to carry out this task so that God would be glorified (Hebrews 13:21). Even those young in age or young in their faith have been given everything they need to tell others about Jesus.

Talk About It

What fears do you have about sharing the Gospel with others? (examples: not knowledgeable enough, fear of what others will think, won't have the right words, etc.)

Apply It

Have everyone write down a fear they have about sharing the Gospel with others. Fold the papers and then have each person pick one. Read the fear then battle it with truth. For example, "I am afraid I don't know enough to answer people's questions. I don't have to be afraid of not knowing enough because God gave us His Word that we can study together." Then, crumble up your paper and throw it away, along with your fears.

How did you do with the Apply It for Week 30?

NOTES

For I am persuaded that neither death nor life, nor angels nor rulers, nor things present nor things to come, nor powers, nor height nor depth, nor any other created thing will be able to separate us from the love of God that is in Christ Jesus our Lord.

Romans 8:38-39

Week 31:

Nothing Can Separate Us

Read It

> For I am persuaded that neither death nor life, nor angels nor rulers, nor things present nor things to come, nor powers, nor height nor depth, nor any other created thing will be able to separate us from the love of God that is in Christ Jesus our Lord.
> Romans 8:38-39

Think About It

The prophets were sent to tell the people to change their ways, to turn away from their sin and turn back to God. God is merciful and patiently waits for us to come to Him. We all sin, but sometimes we go through periods where we are far from God and not living according to His Word. But we are never too far away to turn back to God, and when we do, He is waiting with open arms.

Romans 8:38-39 tells us there is *nothing* that can take away God's love for us. Nothing! This should give us so much hope knowing that there is nothing God can't forgive or make new and there is nothing we could do to cause Him to stop loving us.

Talk About It

Do you struggle with guilt or thinking there are some things in your life that can't be forgiven?

Apply It

Find the oldest thing in your house. Maybe it's a coin or an heirloom. Talk about how this item seemingly has lasted forever. If you know the story behind the item, talk about what it has gone through before it made it to you. We often say things last forever, but we don't really have a concept of what forever is. But God does, and He tells us that His love truly does last forever.

How did you do with the Apply It for Week 31?

NOTES

Learn to do what is good. Pursue justice. Correct the oppressor. Defend the rights of the fatherless. Plead the widow's cause.

Isaiah 1:17

Evangelism

Week 32:
Justice

Read It

> *Learn to do what is good. Pursue justice. Correct the oppressor. Defend the rights of the fatherless. Plead the widow's cause.*
> Isaiah 1:17

Think About It

Have you ever stood up to a bully or included someone who is usually left out? Sometimes the best way to share Jesus with others is by our actions. Doing the right thing, standing up for those who can't stand up for themselves, fighting for what is right, and caring for those who have been abandoned and forgotten can show others more about Jesus than you ever could through your words alone. God will be the final judge, but He has given us permission to try to correct the injustices we see and experience here on earth so that His name would be glorified, and many more people would come to know Him.

Talk About It

Why do you think some people are more likely to believe in and follow Jesus when they see Christians doing what is right opposed to just listening to Christians talk about what is right?

Apply It

Discuss some of the injustices that you see in your neighborhood, school, work, etc. then choose one to do something about it!

Ideas: donate clothing or food to the homeless or a shelter, write a letter to your local or state lawmakers standing up for the rights of others, invite someone over who is usually left out.

How did you do with the Apply It for Week 32?

NOTES

Therefore, whatever you want others to do for you, do also the same for them, for this is the Law and the Prophets.

Matthew 7:12

The Golden Rule

Read It

> *Therefore, whatever you want others to do for you, do also the same for them, for this is the Law and the Prophets.*
> Matthew 7:12

Think About It

The short Book of Obadiah is basically the Bible's version of the adage "what goes around, comes around." Obadiah was a prophet to Edom, and he warned Edom about their pride. They were prideful about their land, power, wealth, wisdom, and allies and God said He would take all those things away from Edom and give them to Israel, the nation Edom had tormented.

When pride sets in, it leads us to believe we can treat others however we want because we are better than them. This is a quick way to lose friends and hurt those around you. If you want to be treated with respect, show respect to others. If you want people to be kind to you, be kind to them. Of course, there are exceptions, but for the most part, people treat you the way you have treated them.

Talk About It

How does today's verse apply to your family – how should parents treat their children while still maintaining boundaries and being responsible? How should children treat their parents and siblings?

Apply It

Have a "Golden Rule" day. Do as many acts of kindness for each other as you can. At the end of the day, discuss how you treated each other and how it made you feel.

How did you do with the Apply It for Week 33?

NOTES

I will praise God's name with song and exalt him with thanksgiving.

Psalm 69:30

Week 34:
Praise Brings Joy

Read It

> *I will praise God's name with song and*
> *exalt him with thanksgiving.*
> *Psalm 69:30*

Think About It

Have you ever been so excited or happy about something that you shouted out with joy? Maybe your team scored the winning touchdown, or you opened the present you've been longing for, or your parents announced you're going on a special vacation. There are many things that bring us joy and sometimes we just can't contain our excitement – we have to scream or sing or do a little dance to express the joy we feel inside.

God wants us to have this kind of joy and excitement when we praise Him. The Psalms are full of songs and poems that were written to praise God. They highlight all the mighty works of God from creation to rescuing His people. They are a way of saying thank you to God and acknowledging how marvelous and amazing He is. When we praise God, whether it is through song, prayer, or anything else, we should do so with excitement and joy as we remember all He has done for us.

Talk About It

What is your favorite song of praise? What stands out to you in the lyrics?

Apply It

Have a karaoke night singing your favorite praise and worship songs.

How did you do with the Apply It for Week 34?

NOTES

Jesus Christ is the same yesterday, today, and forever.

Hebrews 13:8

Week 35:
God Never Changes

Read It

> *Jesus Christ is the same yesterday, today, and forever.*
> *Hebrews 13:8*

Think About It

Life is always changing, and if you're like me, you don't always like change. We like things to feel safe and familiar, and when a big change occurs it can be scary. Sometimes it's not the actual change that's hard, but it's the waiting and unknowing of what's next that can be scary.

No matter what we are going through, we can have hope because we know that nothing comes as a surprise to God. He already knows the changes that are occurring in our lives, and He is prepared to help us walk through them. Even in the hardest moments of our lives, Jesus never leaves us and even in the biggest changes in our lives, Jesus remains the same. His character is perfect, righteous, holy, loving, and just, and He will always be that way.

Talk About It

Take turns talking about the biggest change you've experienced in your life? Consider how you felt – any fears or worries you experienced – and how you handled the change.

Apply It

Try something different this week! Ideas: try new foods, a different hairstyle, take a different route to work or school, go to an art class.

How did you do with the Apply It for Week 35?

NOTES

Rejoice with those who rejoice; weep with those who weep.

Romans 12:15

Week 36:

Jesus Wept

Read It

Rejoice with those who rejoice; weep with those who weep.
Romans 12:15

Think About It

The shortest verse in the Bible is John 11:35, which says, "Jesus wept." This verse is found in the story of Lazarus, one of Jesus's friends who died. Jesus went to where Lazarus was buried, knowing He was about to raise him from the dead, but before Jesus performed this amazing miracle, He paused and cried for His friend. Jesus didn't tell everyone, "Quit crying, it will be OK," instead, He showed empathy when He cried and grieved with His friends.

Sometimes our family and friends will get sad about things and even though we may be able to see that things are going to turn out OK, we should validate their feelings and show that we care about what they are going through. The same is true for when our family or friends experience something exciting, we should rejoice with them and celebrate the good things in their life.

Talk About It

How can you show empathy to one another?

Apply It

Choose one family friend who is either going through something difficult or who is celebrating something great that happened in their life. Invite that person over to weep with them or rejoice with them.

How did you do with the Apply It for Week 36?

NOTES

No foul language should come from your mouth, but only what is good for building up someone in need, so that it gives grace to those who hear.

Ephesians 4:29

Week 37:

Build Each Other Up

Read It

> No foul language should come from your mouth, but only what is good for building up someone in need, so that it gives grace to those who hear.
> Ephesians 4:29

Think About It

If you're honest, there has probably been a time that someone in your family did something that made you so upset or annoyed you so much that you snapped and said something ugly to them. It can be hard to control our speech, but that's exactly what God tells us to do. Our emotions shouldn't change how we treat others or how we speak. God wants us to use our words to build each other up and encourage one another.

Parents, when your children disobey, how do you speak to them? Do you give them words of advice and encouragement that will teach them how to correct their mistakes or do you scream words that bring shame and discouragement?

Children, when your parents correct you or try to talk to you, do you listen with respect, or do you become defensive or annoyed? What about your siblings? Do you use words that help each other, or do you call each other names and put each other down?

Talk About It

What is the most encouraging thing someone in your family has told you?

Apply It

Play a game of Mad Gab or Guess the Gibberish. You can purchase these games or create your own.

How did you do with the Apply It for Week 37?

NOTES

Each person should do as he has decided in his heart – not reluctantly or out of compulsion, since God loves a cheerful giver.

2 Corinthians 9:7

Week 38:

Cheerful Givers

Read It

> *Each person should do as he has decided in his heart – not reluctantly or out of compulsion, since God loves a cheerful giver.*
> *2 Corinthians 9:7*

Think About It

Giving back to God is an act of worship. It is a way to thank God for all He has blessed us with and recognize that everything we have truly belongs to Him. When we give back to God, it shows respect and gratitude to Him, but it also allows us to help others. No matter what we give, God wants us to give with a cheerful heart. The cool part is our offering doesn't just have to be about money. God values when we sacrifice our time, energy, and talents for His glory just as much as He values our monetary contributions. Using your house to host small groups, giving up your time to volunteer at church, or using your talents to serve others are just a few ways you can give back to God. Whatever you offer to God, do so because that is what He has put on your heart.

Talk About It

We all love getting gifts but 2 Corinthians 9:7 encourages us to be cheerful *givers*. How can giving something up make you happy?

Apply It

Have each person name one way they will give an offering to God this week.

How did you do with the Apply It for Week 38?

NOTES

My Father never stops working. And so I work, too.

John 5:17 ICB

Evangelism

Week 39:
Never Stop Working

Read It

> *My Father never stops working. And so I work, too.*
> *John 5:17 ICB*

Think About It

Four hundred years passed from the time the last prophet spoke to when an angel announced the coming Messiah. We don't have any scripture for this period, but there are other historical accounts that help us know what happened during this era. For example, the Hellenization period led to one primary language (Greek) to be used among many groups of people and the rise of the Roman Empire brought intricate road systems which changed trade routes and communication. Even though the Greeks and Romans oppressed God's people during these years of silence, what they accomplished would be vital for the spread of the Gospel. Even when it seemed like God had forgotten His people, He was always working.

God never stops working, so we should never stop working. There is always someone we can share Jesus with. Sometimes it may feel like our efforts are pointless, but we can trust that even when it seems like God isn't there, He is always working and preparing hearts to come to know Him.

Talk About It

What are some ways you can always be working?

Apply It

Plant a bean seed in a clear container. Be sure to water it and give it sunlight as needed. Over the next few days, notice how the roots begin to grow and the plant develops even though on the surface it looks like nothing is happening.

How did you do with the Apply It for Week 39?

NOTES

Do not lie to one another, since you have put off the old self with its practices.

Colossians 3:9

Week 40:
Honesty is the
Best Policy

Read It

> *Do not lie to one another, since you have put off the*
> *old self with its practices.*
> *Colossians 3:9*

Think About It

You may have heard it said that "honesty is the best policy" but what about when being honest might hurt someone's feelings or get you in trouble? God's word is clear, we should tell the truth. Being honest with one another might be hard sometimes, but it is what God wants for our relationships. When we are honest with each other, it helps us grow our trust for one another. It also shows respect and lets others know that we care about them enough to tell the truth, even if it means we have to face consequences.

Honesty is important in all areas of our lives, no matter how big or small. That means we shouldn't cheat on a test or our taxes, lie about eating our vegetables or about who's house we were at, cover up our sadness or our greatest anxieties. Being honest with your family helps them know how to best help you deal with the mistakes and hard things in your life.

Talk About It

Why is it hard to be honest sometimes?

Apply It

Play Two Truths and a Lie. Each person will take turns saying two truths and one lie about themselves or something that happened during their day and the rest of the family has to guess which one is the lie.

How did you do with the Apply It for Week 40?

NOTES

Carry one another's burdens;
in this way you will fulfill
the Law of Christ.

Galatians 6:2

Week 41:
You Can Share the Hard Stuff Too

Read It

> *Carry one another's burdens; in this way you will fulfill the Law of Christ.*
> *Galatians 6:2*

Think About It

As you've gone through this study, you've learned that God wants you to share joy, love, and kindness with others. But God also wants you to share your struggles with others. We were not meant to go through life alone. God has given us our family, friends, and the church as a source of encouragement and help when we go through the hard, scary, confusing, and sad moments of life.

In Matthew 11:28, Jesus says, "Come to me, all of you who are weary and burdened, and I will give you rest." Our peace and joy are found in Christ, not in whatever is going on in our lives. Jesus wants us to come to Him with our problems so that He can give us peace.

Likewise, He wants us to go to others with our struggles so that we can be encouraged and strengthened by other people who love us and love Christ.

Talk About It

How can you share your burdens with others and with Jesus so that you can have peace?

Apply It

Fill a bag with heavy items (weights, canned goods, books, etc.) and have each person try to carry the bag around the house. Talk about how heavy the bag is when you carry it by yourself. Now find a pole or stick (a mop or broom handle will work). Put the pole through the straps of the bag so the bag is centered on the pole. This time have one person hold one side of the pole and another person hold the other side and carry the bag around the house. Talk about how it is easier to carry the bag when you have help.

How did you do with the Apply It for Week 41?

NOTES

You rejoice in this, even though now for a short time, if necessary, you suffer grief in various trials so that the proven character of your faith — more valuable than gold which though perishable, is refined by fire — may result in praise, glory, and honor at the revelation of Jesus Christ.

1 Peter 1:6-7

Week 42:
Be Refined

Read It

> *You rejoice in this, even though now for a short time, if necessary, you suffer grief in various trials so that the proven character of your faith — more valuable than gold which though perishable, is refined by fire — may result in praise, glory, and honor at the revelation of Jesus Christ.*
> *1 Peter 1:6-7*

Think About It

Goldminers don't just find a piece of gold in the ground and immediately start shaping it into a piece of jewelry. Gold must go through a refining process. It is put in fire and melted down to remove all the impurities. Afterwards, it is cooled and reshaped into a solid piece of gold again. Only after it has gone through this process can the piece of gold be made into whatever it is going to become. God tells us that we are like gold. We are valuable but we have impurities and flaws that need to be refined. Sometimes this means we have to go through trials and grief to learn what is pure and right. Though the trials seem unbearable at times, the end result should be praise to God for making us more like Christ.

Talk About It

Talk about some trials you have gone through as a family. What did you learn from these situations?

Apply It

Make a homemade water filter. Clean out a two-liter bottle and then cut the bottle in half. Flip the top half upside down and put it inside the bottom half like a funnel. Place a coffee filter, old bandana, or paper towels in the funnel portion of the bottle. Next, fill the filter with rocks, gravel, sand, charcoal, and/or cotton balls. Pour dirty water into the filter and watch what happens.

How did you do with the Apply It for Week 42?

NOTES

I never stop giving thanks for you as I remember you in my prayers.

Ephesians 1:16

Week 43:
Thankful for Others

Read It

> *I never stop giving thanks for you as I remember you in my prayers.*
> *Ephesians 1:16*

Think About It

When my children were learning to pray, they often said the same thing each time they prayed. Sometimes I wished they would say something different but one thing I loved hearing each time was them thanking God for each member of our family. Even on our hardest days like when I lost my temper, they would thank God for mommy or when one child was being mean to another, they would still thank God for their brother and sister.

There will be days that we hurt each other's feelings and mess up, but we can always be thankful for the family God has given us and the love and joy we get to experience through being together. Family is a gift from God, and we should always remember to tell Him thank you for the good gifts He gives us.

Talk About It

Pray together, thanking God specifically for each person in your family.

Apply It

Take turns naming one thing you are thankful for about each person in your family.

How did you do with the Apply It for Week 43?

NOTES

Be hospitable to one
another without
complaining.

1 Peter 4:9

Evangelism

Week 44:

Happy Hospitality

Read It

> Be hospitable to one another without complaining.
> 1 Peter 4:9

Think About It

My family hosts small group at our house and it is simultaneously one of the things we most look forward to and most dread each week. We love the opportunity to meet with other people in our home to learn about God, but to be honest, it is hard to always be happy about being hospitable. I find myself grumbling about the crumbs kids left throughout the house, my kids complain of their toys being broken or other kids not playing nice, and sometimes it seems like it's more of a hassle than what it's worth.

God tells us to be hospitable without complaining, so how do we do that when the people we're being hospitable to don't seem care about how they treat our house? We have to look past the messes and look at the people. We want to welcome others into our home so that we can love them like Jesus. We want to be an example of how to use the blessings in our life, such as our house, toys, and food to glorify God and be a blessing to others.

Talk About It

How can being hospitable without complaining teach others about Jesus?

Apply It

Open your home to others this week. Ideas: Invite another family over for dinner, a game night, a movie night, etc.

How did you do with the Apply It for Week 44?

☆ ☆ ☆ ☆ ☆

NOTES

...avoid fighting, and to be kind, always showing gentleness to all people.

Titus 3:2

Week 45:
Kind Words

Read It

> ...*avoid fighting, and to be kind, always showing gentleness to all people.*
> *Titus 3:2*

Think About It

Disagreements are bound to come up within a family and when they do, we need to be able to handle them in a respectful way. Just because we disagree about something doesn't mean we need to fight about it. We can share our thoughts and opinions in a kind and gentle way, open to other's viewpoints and considerate of their feelings. This kind of respect requires humility, where we genuinely listen to others instead of just trying to prove our point and recognize that we may be the one who is wrong. Sometimes we are really passionate about something and have a hard time controlling our tone and the words we use when we talk about it. When this is the case, it is OK to agree to walk away for a little bit and come back to the conversation when you are under control and able to speak with kindness and gentleness.

Talk About It

What is the last thing you fought or disagreed about as a family? How well did you handle it? What could you have done differently?

Apply It

Parents: Give your kids a tube of toothpaste and tell them to squeeze out all the toothpaste on a plate. Then, tell them to put all the toothpaste back in the tube. Once they realize this is an impossible task, talk about how our words are like the toothpaste. Once they come out of our mouth, they can't go back it.

How did you do with the Apply It for Week 45?

☆ ☆ ☆ ☆ ☆

NOTES

Just as each one has received a gift, use it to serve others, as good stewards of the varied grace of God.

1 Peter 4:10

Week 46:

Use Your Gifts

Read It

Just as each one has received a gift, use it to serve others, as good stewards of the varied grace of God.
1 Peter 4:10

Think About It

God is kind to give each of us different talents and gifts. While these things may be enjoyable for us to use, the purpose of gifts is to serve others. The cool thing about gifts is that God has many kinds of gifts to give us, so He doesn't expect us to all serve in the same way. If you are a great speaker, then maybe you serve by teaching a class or leading a prayer but if you are very compassionate then maybe you serve best by donating to local charities or volunteering at a shelter. God doesn't value one gift more than another, so we shouldn't either. All gifts and talents are needed to work together to grow His Kingdom.

Sometimes we aren't sure what our gifts are, or we haven't fully developed our gifts and learned how to use them (this is especially true

195

for kids). We should be faithful to ask God to show us what our gifts and talents are and be ready to use them when He does.

Talk About It

What gifts and talents do each of you have? Help each other recognize how you can use these qualities to serve others.

Apply It

Have a talent show to take turns showing off something each of you are good at.

How did you do with the Apply It for Week 46?

NOTES

His master said to him, Well done, good and faithful servant! You were faithful over a few things; I will put you in charge of many things., Share your master's joy.

Matthew 25:23

Week 47:
Share in His Joy

Read It

> *His master said to him, 'Well done, good and faithful servant! You were faithful over a few things; I will put you in charge of many things. Share your master's joy.*
> *Matthew 25:23*

Think About It

What an amazing day it will be when we get to Heaven and hear God say, 'Well done, good and faithful servant! Share in My joy." God gives us many things to bring us joy in this life, but the joy we experience now is just a taste of what Heaven will be like.

In the meantime, we can work faithfully with enthusiasm and diligence now, knowing that it brings our Father joy to see His children obeying His Word. Zephaniah 3:17 says, "The Lord your God is among you, a warrior who saves. He will rejoice over you with gladness. He will be quiet in his love. He will delight in you with singing." When the work God has given to you seems hard, boring, or monotonous, remember that He rejoices over you with gladness when you are obedient to His calling. God, the Creator of all things, sings over *you*.

Talk About It

How does it make you feel knowing that you can bring joy to God by being faithful over the work He has given you?

Apply It

Make care packages for people you know who are sick, injured, or shut-in. This will bring joy to them, to your family, and to God!

NOTES

No temptation has come upon you except what is common to humanity. But God is faithful: he will not allow you to be tempted beyond what you are able, but with the temptation he will also provide the way out so that you may be able to bear it.

1 Corinthians 10:13

Week 48:

Enduring Temptation

Read It

> No temptation has come upon you except what is common to humanity. But God is faithful; he will not allow you to be tempted beyond what you are able, but with the temptation he will also provide the way out so that you may be able to bear it.
> 1 Corinthians 10:13

Think About It

People often say, "God won't give you more than you can handle" and while they mean well, I don't think that is true or what 1 Corinthians 10:13 is saying. Sometimes, God gives us way more than we can handle so that we would learn to grow in our dependence on Him. If we could handle everything on our own, why would we need God? When we face trials and struggles, God is our help and strength. The same is true when we face temptation. *He* is the one who provides a way out. *He* is the reason why we can bear it.

When Jesus was tempted by Satan in the wilderness, each time Satan tried to cause Jesus to sin, Jesus responded with Scripture. He knew what God's Word said was right and He used that to fight temptation. When we are being tempted, we should run to our Father in prayer and ask Him to show us the escape route He has mapped out for us in His Word.

Talk About It

Why is it important to ask God for help when you are being tempted?

Apply It

Play a game of Would You Rather. Take turns asking each other "would you rather _____ or _____?" Talk about how when we face temptation, we always have a choice.

How did you do with the Apply It for Week 48?

NOTES

For you were called to be free, brothers and sisters; only don't use this freedom as an opportunity for the flesh, but serve one another through love.

Galatians 5:13

Evangelism

Week 49:
Free to Love

Read It

> For you were called to be free, brothers and sisters; only
> don't use this freedom as an opportunity for the flesh,
> but serve one another through love.
> Galatians 5:13

Think About It

Jesus fulfilled every law that God had ever given His people and because of this, we are no longer required to live under the Law. We are given the freedom to eat, drink, and do anything so long as it is for God's glory (1 Corinthians 10:31). However, just because we have the freedom to do something, doesn't mean we should. Maybe there are words you are allowed to say or foods you are allowed to eat but your friend isn't. When you are with that friend, you shouldn't use those words or eat those foods because it might cause your friend to break the rules for their family. Even though God has given us great freedom through Jesus, we should use that freedom to love others and not do things that might cause them to disobey.

Talk About It

Can you think of any other examples of things that you have the freedom to do but shouldn't so that you can love others well?

Apply It

Read through some of the Old Testament Laws that said what kinds of foods the Israelites could and could not eat. Try to follow those rules for the week. At the end of the week, talk about the freedoms we have in Christ and how we can enjoy them while still respecting and serving others in love.

How did you do with the Apply It for Week 49?

☆ ☆ ☆ ☆ ☆

NOTES

With all humility and gentleness, with patience, bearing with one another in love.

Ephesians 4:2

Week 50:
Bear with One Another

Read It

> *With all humility and gentleness, with patience,*
> *bearing with one another in love.*
> *Ephesians 4:2*

Think About It

I don't know how many times I have asked God to give me patience and then completely miss the opportunities He gave me to practice patience. It is hard to be patient when our child repeatedly disobeys, or when we have to listen to our dad's jokes, or when our little sister wants to play the longest game in the history of games! But being patient in these moments is an opportunity to love our family.

God tells us to "bear with one another in love." This means sometimes we do things we don't really enjoy to show love to others. It also means that patience is something we will have to practice over and over if we want to get better at it. When you find yourself struggling to

211

be patient with others, remember it is an opportunity to show love and respect.

Talk About It

When is it most difficult for you to be patient?

Apply It

Do a puzzle together that will be challenging for your family because it has a lot of pieces or because it has a difficult pattern or odd shape. See how long it takes you to complete the puzzle. Did anyone get frustrated or upset at any point?

How did you do with the Apply It for Week 50?

NOTES

In the same way the Spirit also helps us in our weakness, because we do not know what to pray for as we should, but the Spirit himself intercedes for us with inexpressible groanings.

Romans 8:26

Week 51:
We Have a Helper for Prayer

Read It

> *In the same way the Spirit also helps us in our weakness,*
> *because we do not know what to pray for as we should,*
> *but the Spirit himself intercedes for us*
> *with inexpressible groanings.*
> *Romans 8:26*

Think About It

1 Thessalonians 5:17 tells us to "pray constantly" but sometimes we're not sure what to pray for or how to pray. There are actually many different types of prayers we can pray – prayers of praise and adoration, thanksgiving, lament, petition, confession, guidance, intercession, and more! God wants us to come to Him with everything, the good and the bad. He doesn't expect us to have the perfect words prepared when we come to Him, He just wants to hear what is on our hearts. If that's not comforting enough, God tells us that the Spirit helps us pray. Even

215

when we feel confused and don't know what to pray for or when we are so upset that we can't speak, the Spirit takes what is on our heart and delivers it to God for us.

Talk About It

Is prayer ever hard for you? How does it make you feel knowing that God wants to help you pray?

Apply It

Be intentional about listening to how other people pray. Listen carefully to the words they use and the things they pray for. While we certainly have the Spirit to help us pray, sometimes we can learn a lot about prayer by listening to other people pray.

How did you do with the Apply It for Week 51?

NOTES

Love is patient, love is kind. Love does not envy, is not boastful, is not arrogant, is not rude, is not self-seeking, is not irritable, and does not keep a record of wrongs. Love finds no joy in unrighteousness but rejoices in the truth. It bears all things, believes all things, hopes all things, endures all things. Love never ends.

1 Corinthians 13:4-8

Week 52:

Love Is...

Read It

> Love is patient, love is kind. Love does not envy, is not
> boastful, is not arrogant, is not rude, is not self-seeking, is
> not irritable, and does not keep a record of wrongs.
> Love finds no joy in unrighteousness but rejoices in the truth.
> It bears all things, believes all things, hopes all things,
> endures all things. Love never ends.
> 1 Corinthians 13:4-8

Think About It

You've made it to the end of this year-long devotional and we're ending with the same scripture that we began with in the introduction – 1 Corinthians 13:4-8. These verses encompass the core values that are essential to Christian families who want to grow in their love and affection for one another and for God.

Talk About It

Over the last year, which of these characteristics of love has your family done well? Which ones are a struggle? Where have you seen the most improvement?

Apply It

Take turns talking about what you liked the most about this study and how it has impacted your relationships with one another.

How did you do with the Apply It for Week 52?

Topical Index

Loving Kindness

Joy

Respect

Evangelism

Scripture Index

Evangelism

About the Author

Kailey Lentsch is a Christian author and freelance writer. Her goal is to incorporate her life experience with sound biblical theology to provide readers with Christ-centered information and advice. Kailey was born and raised in Ocala, Florida, where she currently lives with her husband and their three children. She has a master's degree in social work from the University of Central Florida. Kailey serves her local church by developing children's curriculum and previously worked as a community social worker and special education teacher. Through her experience working with children in the education system, at church, and with her own children, Kailey recognized a need for age-appropriate faith-based instruction for youth. She believes that teaching children about Jesus at an early age sets the foundation for strong faith and a Christ-centered life.

About the Publisher

Triune Publications is a faith-based publication dedicated to spreading God's word. Founded in 2021, Triune Publications is determined to do its part in the great commission. To go into all the world and preach the good news of the gospel to all people. As we continue that endeavor, we hope our material brings healing, salvation, community, unity, and a stronger relationship with God. We are so blessed to have this opportunity and would like to thank you for choosing this book. We hope it brings you closer to God and strengthens your walk with the Lord. Thank you, and God Bless.

A Special Thank You

Thank you for reading our family devotional. Before you go, we ask that you please leave a review wherever you purchased our material. It would mean a lot to us and help us continue to provide wonderful faith-based material for you in the future.

Thank you and God Bless,
The Triune Publications Team

Made in the USA
Columbia, SC
05 January 2025

51286051R00126